HEINEMANN STATE STUDIES

Uniquely
Oklahoma

Reuben Anderson

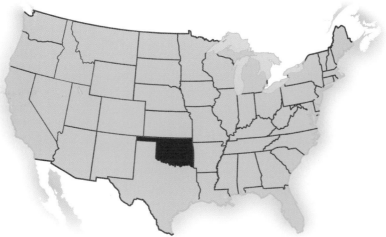

Heinemann Library
Chicago, Illinois

Designed by Heinemann Library
Printed in China by WKT Company Limited.

08 07 06 05 04
10 9 8 7 6 5 4 3 2 1

**Library of Congress
Cataloging-in-Publication Data**

Anderson, J. Christopher.
    Uniquely Oklahoma / J. Christopher Anderson.
        p. cm.--(Heinemann state studies)
Includes bibliographical references and index.
    ISBN 1-4034-4658-X (lib. bdg.)--
ISBN 1-4034-4727-6 (pbk.)
    1. Oklahoma--Juvenile literature. [1. Oklahoma.]
I. Title. II. Series.
    F694.3.A53 2004
    976.6'054--dc22

                                            2003025720

Cover Pictures

Top (left to right) Oklahoma City National
Memorial, Oklahoma state flag, state capitol,
Oklahoma Land Rush **Main** oil field

Acknowledgments
Development and photo research by
BOOK BUILDERS LLC

The author and publishers are grateful to the
following for permission to reproduce copyrighted
material:

Cover photographs by (top, L-R) Chuck Pefley/
Alamy; Joe Sohm/Alamy; Joe Sohm/Alamy; Culver
(main) Pictor International/Image State/Alamy

Title page (L-R): Courtesy Oklahoma City
Convention and Visitors Bureau; Brand X
Pictures/Alamy; Contents: Courtesy Oklahoma
Tourism; p. 4, 17, 28 Courtesy Oklahoma City
Convention and Visitors Bureau; p. 5 Courtesy U.S.
Army; p. 6, 12T, 12B, 13M, 13B, 14T, 15T, 29, 36,
39, 41, 43 Courtesy Oklahoma Tourism; p. 7 Stock
Connection, Inc./Alamy; p. 8, 42, 45 IMA for
BOOK BUILDERS LLC; p. 10 Courtesy NASA;
p. 11T Joe Sohm/Alamy; p. 11B One Mile Up; p.
13T Paul Wray/Forestry Images; p. 14M Robert A.
Karges/USFWS; p. 14B Gary M. Stolz/USFWS;
p. 15B Ron Singer/USFWS; p. 19 AP Photo; p. 20
AP/Wide World Photo; p. 21T AP Photo; p. 21B
Dennis Cook/AP Photo; p. 22T Nick Ut/AP Photo;
p. 22B Wayne Hacker/Warren Image/Alamy; p. 24
Culver; p. 25 Courtesy Governor's Office; p. 27 Joe
Sohm/Alamy; p. 31 Courtesy Paul Schatte/Head
Country Barbecue Team, Ponca City; p. 32T The
Great American Stock/Index Stock Imagery; p. 32B
Courtesy Elvin Godbehere Collection; p. 34 R.
Capozzelli/Heinemann Library; p. 35T Courtesy
Oklahoma Redhawks; p. 35B AP Photo; p. 37
Brand X Pictures/Alamy; p. 38 Pictor
International/Image State/Alamy; p. 40 Chuck
Pefley/Alamy; p. 41T Courtesy of ASA National
Softball Hall of Fame, Oklahoma City; p. 44
Courtesy Will Rogers Memorial Museum.

Special thanks to Dr. William Blackburn of the
Oklahoma Historical Society for his expert
comments in the preparation of this book.

Every effort has been made to contact copyright
holders of any material reproduced in this book.
Any omissions will be rectified in subsequent
printings if notice is given to the publisher.

Some words are shown in bold, **like this.**
You can find out what they mean by looking
in the glossary.

Contents

Uniquely Oklahoma

Oklahoma is unique, a one-of-a-kind state. It is the only state that began as a territory promised to Native Americans but was then opened for further settlement by the **federal government.** Oklahoma has the largest Native American population of any state—more than 250,000. The state is the headquarters of 39 different tribes. Oklahoma is located in the Midwestern United States. It is bordered to the east by Missouri and Arkansas, to the south by Texas, to the west by New Mexico, and to the north by Colorado and Kansas.

ORIGIN OF THE STATE'S NAME

Allen Wright, a missionary who worked among the Choctaw, is believed to have combined two Choctaw words, *okla,* meaning people, and *homma,* meaning red, into *Oklahoma.* Thus, Oklahoma means "red people" in the Choctaw language. The Choctaw was the first tribe that the U.S. government moved to what is today Oklahoma. The tribe's original home was in present-day Mississippi and Alabama.

Oklahoma City is the nation's third-largest city in area, covering nearly 650 square miles.

MAJOR CITIES

Oklahoma City was founded in the **land rush** of 1889. Located near the center of the state, Oklahoma City is the state's largest cityIn 1910, when Oklahoma City was named the capital of Oklahoma, the city's population was about 64,000. Today, the city is home to more than 500,000 people. Oklahoma City is the only state capital located on an oil field.

Tulsa, which was founded in 1882, was once called the "oil capital of the world." Oil was first struck near Tulsa in 1901, and the town's population soared. Today, with a population of almost 400,000, it is the second-largest city in Oklahoma. Tulsa is sometimes called "T-Town" because it was named after Tulsey Town, a Cherokee town in Alabama.

Lawton was formed in 1901 during a **land lottery** in which people won 160 acres of land if their name was drawn. Today, the population in Lawton is more than 90,000. The Fort Sill military base, which is located near Lawton, houses "Atomic Annie," a 280-millimeter cannon. Atomic Annie is the world's first **atomic cannon.** Each August Native American people from many tribes come to the city of Anadarko, near Lawton. Anadarko holds one of the largest gatherings of the Plains peoples. Because so many Native American tribes have lived in Anadarko, it is known as the "Indian Capital of the Nation."

Founded in 1869, Fort Sill is still an active military base.

Oklahoma's Geography and Climate

Oklahoma is mostly a land of flat, rich **plains** and low hills. Geographers divide Oklahoma into ten land regions.

LAND

The Ozark **Plateau** is in northeastern Oklahoma. Many rivers flow through this region, and wide areas of flat land stretch between the rivers. To the west and south of the Ozark Plateau is the Prairie Plains. This region produces most of the state's coal and much of its oil.

In the southeastern part of Oklahoma, on the border with Arkansas, are the Ouachita Mountains. These sandstone ridges run east to west. The Ouachita Mountains make up the roughest land in the state. In the north-central part of Oklahoma, extending south from the Kansas border to the Red River, is the Sandstone Hills Region. The Sandstone Hills reach from 250 to 400 feet high. The Arbuckle Mountains make up a small area of about 1,000 square miles in south-central Oklahoma.

The Arbuckle Mountains are low mountains that rise about 600 to 700 feet above the plains.

The Wichita Mountains, in southwestern Oklahoma, are among the oldest mountains on earth. In 1901, President William McKinley set aside the Wichita Mountains as a forest preserve, and in 1935, the area became a part of the National Wildlife Refuge System. The Wichita Mountains Wildlife Refuge is the oldest managed wildlife area in the United States.

Oklahoma ranks second in the United States in the number of tornadoes that occur each year.

The Red River Valley Region, in southern Oklahoma along the Texas border, is rolling **prairie.** Cotton, peanuts, and vegetables grow in this region's sandy and fertile soil.

To the west of the Sandstone Hills are the Red Beds Plains. The largest land region in Oklahoma, the Red Beds Plains stretch south from the Kansas border through the center of the state. The Red Beds Plains rise upward from east to west.

The Gypsum Hills lie west of the Red Beds Plains and extend north to the High Plains in the northwestern part of the state. The Gypsum Hills are low hills and are capped with fifteen- to twenty-foot layers of **gypsum.** Because of their gypsum content, the Gypsum Hills sparkle in the sunlight and are sometimes called the Glass Hills. People use gypsum in paint and cement.

The High Plains, in northwestern Oklahoma, are flat, level grasslands. The High Plains rise from about 2,000 feet above sea level in the east to 4,973 feet above sea level at Black Mesa in the west. This region is in the Oklahoma Panhandle, the thin strip of land 166 miles long and 34 miles wide.

CLIMATE

Oklahoma has long, hot, somewhat **humid** summers and relatively mild winters. In the summer, temperatures are usually between 80°F and 90°F, while in the winter temperatures often dip to between 30°F and 40°F during the day.

During the summer months when cool air from the Rocky Mountains collides with warm air from the Gulf of Mexico, severe thunderstorms are created. These storms can produce tornadoes. These violent, spinning, funnel-shaped clouds are common in Oklahoma during the spring and summer months.

The panhandle in the northwest is the driest part of Oklahoma. It receives less than twenty inches of precipitation each year.

Average Annual Precipitation Oklahoma

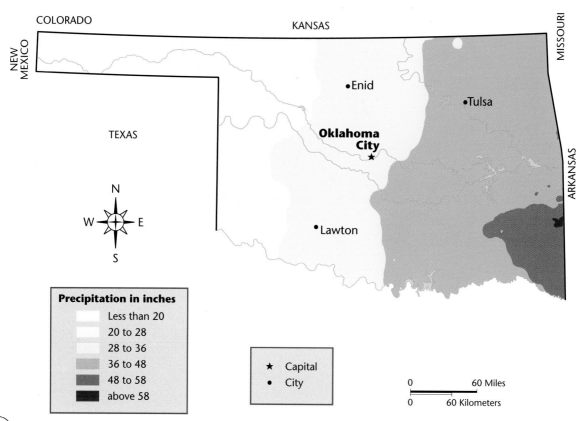

COLORADO

KANSAS

MISSOURI

NEW MEXICO

•Enid

•Tulsa

TEXAS

Oklahoma City
★

ARKANSAS

N
W E
S

•Lawton

Precipitation in inches

	Less than 20
	20 to 28
	28 to 36
	36 to 48
	48 to 58
	above 58

★ Capital
• City

0   60 Miles

0   60 Kilometers

8

Famous Firsts

William Wrigley manufactured his first stick of chewing gum in Guthrie in 1892. Today, Wrigley's gum is sold throughout the world. In the United States, Wrigley's sales total more than $2 billion each year.

In 1921, Earl Hull founded WKY radio, the first AM radio station to broadcast west of the Mississippi River. The station broadcast from Hull's home in Oklahoma City.

Carl C. Magee invented the world's first automatic parking meter. He installed it in Oklahoma City in 1935. At the time, Magee was a member of the Oklahoma City Chamber of Commerce. He and other members were concerned that workers were leaving their cars on the city streets all day, leaving no parking spaces for shoppers or tourists. Magee came up with the idea of charging for the parking places. The idea caught on, and now parking meters are used throughout the world.

Bob Dunn, a musician from Beggs, invented the first electric guitar in 1935. Electric guitars became very popular in the 1950s and 1960s with the rise of rock-and-roll music.

In 1935, Sylvan N. Goldman invented the first shopping cart for his Standard and Humpty Dumpty grocery stores. At first, the carts were not popular. People were used to carrying their groceries. Some shoppers were already pushing baby carriages and could not push a cart as well. Goldman persuaded shoppers to use the carts by hiring people of all ages to walk around the store pushing carts, pretending to shop.

Astronaut Thomas P. Stafford, who was born in Weatherford in 1930, is in the *Guinness Book of World Records* as the world's fastest traveling man. He piloted a reentry at 24,791 miles per hour aboard *Apollo X*.

More astronauts come from Oklahoma than from any other state. These astronauts include Gordon Cooper from Shawnee, Owen K. Garriott from Enid, and Shannon Lucid, who was born in China but considers Bethany her hometown.

In May 1969, Thomas Stafford commanded Apollo X *on an eight-day space mission that brought back information about the surface of the moon.*

In 1948, at Tinkers Air Force Base, Captain Robert C. Miller and Major Ernest J. Fawbush issued the nation's first tornado warning, predicting a tornado would hit Oklahoma. The prediction was correct. The tornado caused considerable destruction, including $6 million in damage to Tinkers Air Force Base. Today, tornado watches and warnings save lives across the nation.

Oklahoma's State Symbols

OKLAHOMA STATE FLAG

Warriors of the Osage tribe, who moved to what is now Oklahoma in the 1700s, carried a shield similar to the one pictured on the Oklahoma state flag. The pipe and olive branch are symbols of peace. The small crosses on the flag stand for stars.

The Oklahoma state flag was adopted in 1925.

OKLAHOMA STATE SEAL

The state seal of Oklahoma is in the shape of a star. The five points represent the five Native American nations that first settled in what is now Oklahoma—the Cherokee, Choctaw, Chickasaw, Seminole, and Creek. The 45 stars on the seal represent the 45 states that entered the Union before Oklahoma became the 46th state.

STATE MOTTO: *LABOR OMNIA VINCIT*

Oklahoma's state motto is Latin for "Labor conquers all things." It reflects the belief that with hard work, all things are possible.

The state seal was adopted in 1907, the same year Oklahoma became a state.

STATE NICKNAME: SOONER STATE

Oklahoma is called the Sooner State because some people were so eager to acquire land in what is now Oklahoma in 1889 that they arrived sooner than the federal government told them that they could.

"Oklahoma!"

Oklahoma, where the wind comes
 sweepin' down the plain
And the wavin' wheat can sure smell
 sweet
When the wind comes right behind
 the rain.
Oklahoma, Ev'ry night my honey lamb
 and I
Sit alone and talk and watch a hawk
Makin' lazy circles in the sky.

We know we belong to the land
And the land we belong to is grand!
And when we say
Yeeow! Ayipioeeay!
We're only sayin'
You're doin' fine, Oklahoma!
Oklahoma O.K.

*Mistletoe is not a flower. It is actually a **parasite** that grows on trees and feeds off them.*

STATE SONG: "OKLAHOMA!"

Oklahoma's state song is from the Richard Rogers and Oscar Hammerstein musical *Oklahoma!* The title song was adopted in 1953 by the state legislature. The musical, which opened in New York on March 31, 1943, introduced the state and its history to many theatergoers.

STATE FLOWER: MISTLETOE

Oklahomans chose mistletoe as their flower in 1893, fourteen years before statehood. It grows throughout southern Oklahoma.

STATE WILDFLOWER: INDIAN BLANKET

Oklahoma's lawmakers adopted the Indian blanket flower as the state wildflower to honor Oklahoma's Native American heritage. According to a Cherokee legend, an elderly Native American man made colorful blankets. When he was ready to die, he made one last blanket for himself. When the man died, he

Oklahoma's legislature adopted the Indian blanket flower as the state wildflower in 1910.

was wrapped in the blanket and buried. In the spring, wildflowers in the same colors as his blanket covered the ground from May to August.

STATE TREE: REDBUD

In 1937, the legislature made the redbud tree the official state tree. The tree grows in the valleys, forests, and **plains** of Oklahoma.

Each spring redbud trees bloom with small clusters of pink flowers before their glossy green leaves emerge.

STATE BIRD: SCISSOR-TAILED FLYCATCHER

The scissor-tailed flycatcher became the state bird in 1951. The legislature chose it because its breeding grounds are found throughout Oklahoma. At the same time, the legislature declared May 1 as Bird Day, a day for people to promote the preservation of wildlife.

The scissor-tailed flycatcher is known for its long tail feathers.

STATE FISH: WHITE BASS

Lawmakers named the white bass the state fish in 1974. The fish, also known as the sand bass, can be found in open water in either shallow or deep areas.

The largest sand bass caught and recorded in Oklahoma's history weighed five pounds, fourteen ounces.

The American buffalo can weigh up to 2,000 pounds, run up to 40 miles an hour, and reach 6 feet high at the shoulder.

STATE ANIMAL: AMERICAN BUFFALO

The American buffalo, or bison, was important to the Native Americans and other settlers on the Oklahoma plains. The buffalo supplied meat, and its hide provided clothing and shelter. It was adopted as the state animal in 1972.

The male collard lizard is more colorful than the female.

STATE REPTILE: COLLARD LIZARD

Nicknamed the "mountain boomer," the collard lizard became the state reptile in 1969. Collard lizards are most often found in the hilly, rocky areas of Oklahoma.

STATE GAME BIRD: WILD TURKEY

The wild turkey was named Oklahoma's official game bird in 1990. By the late 1940s, wild turkeys were nearly **extinct** in Oklahoma because of over-hunting.

When fully grown, the male turkey, called a tom, can stand up to three feet tall, be four feet long, and weigh more than twenty pounds.

Conservation efforts in all 77 of Oklahoma's counties have made hunting the wild birds possible once again.

STATE ROCK: ROSE ROCK

Rose rock is the popular name for the mineral barite, which forms rock crystals in the shape of roses. The legislature adopted barite as the state rock in 1968.

STATE INSECT: HONEYBEE

The legislature named the honeybee Oklahoma's state insect in 1992. Oklahoma produces about 300,000 pounds of honey each year.

One of the largest clusters of rose rock in Oklahoma was discovered near Norman. The cluster weighed almost 800 pounds and measured 62 inches long, 24 inches high, and 18 inches wide.

STATE BUTTERFLY: BLACK SWALLOWTAIL

The butterfly plays an important role in the **pollination** of flowers. The legislature adopted the black swallowtail as the state butterfly in 1996 for its beauty and ability to help plants bloom.

The black swallowtail calls Oklahoma home from May to October.

STATE GRASS: INDIAN GRASS

Indian grass grows on the grasslands of Oklahoma, where livestock and wild animals feed on its leaves. Indian grass became the state grass in 1972.

Oklahoma's History and People

Oklahoma is a land that many people have called home. Native Americans and European settlers from many countries have contributed to the state.

EARLY PEOPLES

The first known people to live in what is now Oklahoma were hunter-gatherers. Near Anadarko, **archaeologists** have found bones of woolly **mammoths** that these early people hunted, as well as parts of the spears they used as weapons. Scientists believe that these people lived more than 11,000 years ago.

Outside the town of Spiro are twelve large earthen mounds. These mounds were part of a city used by pre-historic peoples from about 850 to 1450. Nine of the mounds were used to house the people of the area. Two other mounds were used as temples. The remaining mound was used as a burial site. The Spiro Mounds became known as an important **archaeological** site when the first dig took place in the area in 1917.

EUROPEAN EXPLORERS

The area's first written history began in 1541 when the Spanish explorer Francisco Vásquez de Coronado and his crew wrote about their explorations in the area. They were searching for a lost city of gold, of which the natives in Mexico had spoken. Coronado found Osage and Kiowa peoples living in the area, but no gold. Coronado claimed the land for the Spanish king.

French explorers visited the area after the Spanish. The French were not searching for gold. They wanted to trade furs and **pelts.** Coming south from Canada, the French rode in canoes down the Mississippi, the Red, and the Arkansas rivers. In 1719, Bernard de La Harpe became the first French explorer to arrive in the area. The French also claimed the land that became Oklahoma, as well as all the land drained by the Mississippi River, naming the area Louisiana in honor of the French king, Louis XIV.

In 1803, the United States purchased the **Louisiana Territory** from France for $15 million. Thus, most of what is now Oklahoma became a part of the United States. By the time of the Louisiana Purchase, the Osage, Cherokee, Quapaw, and other tribes also lived in the area.

NATIVE AMERICAN TERRITORY

In 1830, the U.S. Congress passed the Indian Removal Act. This law stated that Native Americans living east of the Mississippi River would be forced to move to what is today Oklahoma. This land, which was called Indian Territory, was set aside for the Native Americans. Within the territory, the **federal government** established areas for several Native American tribes.

In 1838, the Cherokee people were moved by U.S. soldiers from Georgia to the Indian Territory. Men, women, and children were taken from towns and farms in Georgia and forced to walk all the way to Oklahoma. Nearly 4,000 Cherokees died on

The End of the Trail (1915) *by James Earle Fraser is a famous sculpture that reminds people of the sadness of the Trail of Tears.*

this journey, which has become known as the Trail of Tears.

LAND RUSH

The **land rush** of 1889 opened up areas of what would become Oklahoma to white settlers. These settlers waited to stake claims in parts of Oklahoma that had not been given to a Native American tribe. Each settler to stake an area was entitled to a square-mile plot of land. At noon on April 22, 1889, buglers sounded the beginning of the first land rush. However, when the pioneers rushed into the area, they were surprised to find white settlers already living there. These early settlers became known as Sooners because they crossed into the territory too soon—before the official beginning of the land rush. Oklahoma became known as the Sooner State because of these early settlers. In 1890, Congress established the Oklahoma Territory for the white settlers.

STATEHOOD

Soon after becoming a territory, the people of Oklahoma wanted statehood. In 1891, they held a statehood convention requesting that the Oklahoma Territory and Indian Territory be joined into one state. The leaders of the Indian Territory opposed this plan. In response, some white Oklahomans began to call for separate statehood for Oklahoma. In August 1905, Native American leaders met in Muskogee to write a constitution for a new state, named Sequoyah, to be made up of only Indian Territory. The Sequoyah Constitution was submitted, but Congress took no action on it. Finally, in June 1906, Congress passed a bill that provided for the admission of Oklahoma and the Indian Territory into the Union as one state. Guthrie was named the temporary capital.

OKLAHOMA IN THE 1900s

Oklahoma grew quickly in the early 1900s as people moved to the state, hoping to strike it rich in the oil fields. Oil booms occurred near Tulsa (1905), Chushing (1912), Siminola (1923), and Oklahoma City (1928).

In the 1930s, Oklahoma and other areas of the southern plains fell on hard times. This area of the country became known as the Dust Bowl. Poor farming practices and years of **drought** caused the Dust Bowl. In the past, when rainfall was good, the land produced plentiful crops. But as the droughts of the early 1930s became worse, the farmers kept plowing and planting, but nothing would grow. The roots of the native grasses, which held the soil in place, were gone. The plains winds whipped across the fields, raising clouds of dust, which would drift like snow, covering the farms. Many Oklahomans moved west in search of work.

Fields in western Oklahoma lost fertile topsoil during the Dust Bowl era of the 1930s.

Oklahoma City Bombing

On April 19, 1995, the Alfred P. Murrah building in Oklahoma City was bombed by Timothy McVeigh, a U.S. citizen. A total of 168 people died, including many children who were at a daycare center in the building. The bombing was the worst act of **terrorism** committed on U.S. soil up to that time. McVeigh and an accomplice were convicted for their crime in 1997. Today, an outdoor memorial, which is open 24 hours a day, 365 days a year, stands where the Murrah building once stood.

FAMOUS PEOPLE

Will Rogers (1879–1935), entertainer. Will Rogers was born on a large ranch in Cherokee Territory near what would later be called Oologah. Rogers, who was part Cherokee, was skilled at lassoing cattle. He worked for a time as a cowboy and later became a Broadway star in the 1920s and 1930s, a popular broadcaster, and the author of more than 4,000 newspaper columns. Rogers, who died in a plane crash in 1935, is remembered for his witty sense of humor.

Chester Gould (1900–1985), cartoonist. Born in Pawnee, Chester Gould's first comic strip appeared in a newspaper, the *Hearst Syndicate,* in 1924. Gould went on to create the popular detective Dick Tracy.

Woody Guthrie (1912–1967), folk singer, composer. Woodrow Wilson Guthrie, known as Woody Guthrie, was born in the frontier town of Okemah. He began his singing career with a band called the Corn Cob Trio.

Ralph Ellison's work was influenced by the frontier.

Unable to support his family through the hard times of the Dust Bowl years, Guthrie moved to California, where he continued singing. He later wrote "The Dust Bowl Ballads," which were songs that told of the hardships of that time. Guthrie also published an autobiography, *Bound for Glory*, about his experiences during the Great Depression.

Ralph Ellison (1914–1994), writer. Ralph Ellison was born in Oklahoma City. His first novel, *The Invisible Man,* was published in 1952. Ellison wrote of his own experiences, as well as those of other African Americans.

John Berryman (1914–1972), poet. Born in McAlester, John Berryman wrote several books of poetry. His 1964 book, *77 Dream Songs,* won a **Pulitzer Prize.**

Maria Tallchief (1925–   ), ballerina. Of Osage heritage, Maria Tallchief was born in Fairfax. As a young woman, Tallchief studied ballet in Kansas City. She quickly became a famous dancer. Admired by millions of fans, President Dwight Eisenhower declared her "Woman of the Year" in 1953. After her dancing career, she became a dance instructor.

Maria Tallchief was the leading ballerina of the New York City Ballet during the 1950s.

Mickey Mantle (1931–1995), baseball player. Mickey Mantle was born in Spavinaw, but he and his family moved to Commerce when he was three years old. Mantle played in twelve World Series with the New York Yankees. Known for his hitting, Mantle hit 536 career home runs.

Wilma Mankiller (1945–   ), Cherokee chief. Wilma Mankiller was born in Tahlequah. In 1985, Mankiller was elected chief of the Cherokee tribe, the second-largest Native American tribe in the United States, with more than 140,000 members. Mankiller is the first woman to serve as chief of a tribe. She was inducted into the Oklahoma Hall of Fame for her contributions to Native Americans in the state, particularly her work for healthcare and children's rights.

Wilma Mankiller brought native wisdom, culture, and spirituality to her role as tribal leader.

In 1999, Ron Howard was given a star in front of Mann's Chinese Theatre in Los Angeles for his accomplishments in film and television.

Johnny Bench (1947–), baseball player. Johnny Bench was born in Oklahoma City. Bench played catcher for the Cincinnati Reds and was elected to the Baseball Hall of Fame in 1989.

Ron Howard (1954–), actor and director. Born in Duncan, Ron Howard began acting as a child. He played Opie on the TV show, *The Andy Griffith Show,* and starred in *Happy Days.* As an adult, Howard became a well-known movie director.

Vince Gill (1957–), singer. Vince Gill was born in Norman. He is a well-known country-music performer and has won 14 Grammy awards. Among his hits are "Oklahoma Borderline" and "When I Call Your Name."

Garth Brooks has sold more than 100 million albums over the last decade.

Garth Brooks (1962–), singer. Born in Tulsa, Garth Brooks is a country-music performer. One of his albums, *Double Live,* is the highest selling live album in music history. In 2001, Brooks set a record for the most times an artist's album was released at number one on the music charts.

The Oklahoma Land Rush!

On March 2, 1889, President Grover Cleveland signed into law a **bill** that opened land in Oklahoma to white settlers. The bill also said that the land in the Oklahoma Territory would be free.

DISREGARD FOR NATIVE AMERICAN CLAIMS

The land in the Oklahoma Territory had been set aside for Native Americans. In the 1870s, a Cherokee lawyer, Colonel Elias Boudinot, pointed out to the U.S. government that two million acres of land were not assigned to any tribe. Many people wanted this remaining land for Native Americans, but the government decided to open the land to white settlers.

THE LAND GRAB

The first of five land rushes was set to begin at noon on April 22, 1889. According to the land rush rules, no one could claim any land until after a bugle sounded. Then, person could claim 160 acres by pounding a small wooden stake into the ground. The settlers were then to form towns or farms with their land. Families lined up at the border days in advance, and many people stayed in tents or huts as they waited.

When the bugle sounded at noon, about 50,000 people raced into the Oklahoma Territory and staked claims to farms or small-town lots. Entire cities, such as Guthrie, were claimed within a single day. People came from all over the United States, as well as from countries such as Poland, Germany, and Ireland for the free land.

Horses were very valuable during the land rush. Those who did not have one were forced to run to find their claims.

"JUMPING THE GUN"

But some people crossed the border before the bugle sounded. These people became known as Sooners because they staked their claims too soon. Some were government workers who crossed the line early to **survey** the land and then pretended that they were the first settlers to arrive. The settlers who arrived early gave Oklahoma its nickname, the Sooner State.

No Man's Land: The Oklahoma Panhandle

After the land rushes, the panhandle of Oklahoma did not have a government. According to a law known as the Compromise of 1850, the area did not belong to any state. Without a government, the panhandle attracted cattle thieves and other outlaws. Their activities led many to call the panhandle "no man's land." During a drought in the 1880s, farmers and ranchers from Kansas also went to live in the panhandle. They built small villages, and towns such as Borger were created as these people began to trade with one another. The area soon needed a government. In 1890 Congress made "no man's land" a part of the Oklahoma Territory.

Oklahoma's State Government

Oklahoma's government is based in Oklahoma City, the capital. The state is governed by a **constitution,** a plan of government approved by the state's people.

The state's constitution was written in 1907, the year Oklahoma became a state. It promises many freedoms for Oklahoma's people, including freedom of religion, speech, and the press. These basic rights are based on those listed in the U.S. Constitution.

Oklahoma's government is similar to the **federal government** in Washington, D.C. Like the federal government, Oklahoma's government is made up of three branches—the legislative, the executive, and the judicial branch.

In 2004, Governor Brad Henry worked to reduce teen smoking.

THE LEGISLATIVE BRANCH

Oklahoma's **legislature** consists of two houses—the senate and the house of representatives. The senate's 48 members are elected to 4-year terms. The house's 101 members are elected to 2-year terms. In Oklahoma, senators and representatives can serve no more than twelve years total.

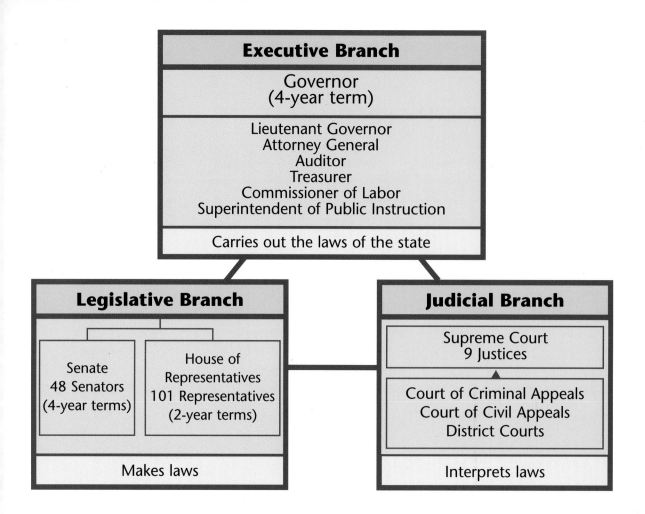

A **bill,** or proposed law, may start in either house of the legislature. After most bills have been approved by a majority, or more than half, of the members of both houses, they are sent to the governor. If the governor signs the bill, it becomes a law. If the governor vetoes, or rejects, the bill, it becomes law only if a majority of the legislature votes to override the veto.

THE EXECUTIVE BRANCH

The executive branch enforces the state's laws and runs the state from day to day. The governor is the head of this branch. The lieutenant governor is the second-highest state official. The lieutenant governor acts as a replacement if the governor is unable to fulfill the duties of the office. Voters elect these two government leaders to a four-year term of office. The governor is limited to two four-year terms.

Voters also elect six other major officials in the executive branch to four-year terms. The treasurer collects the state's tax money. The auditor oversees how the state's money is spent. The attorney general serves as the state's legal adviser. The commissioner of labor helps workers, and the insurance commissioner helps people receive fair treatment from insurance companies. The superintendent of public instruction oversees the state's schools.

Construction on the capitol in Oklahoma City began in 1914, and lawmakers moved into the building in 1917. Construction on the capitol's dome did not begin until 2000 and was finished in 2002.

THE JUDICIAL BRANCH

The judicial branch decides how the state's laws apply to particular cases. The Oklahoma court system is made up of the supreme court, the court of criminal appeals, the court of civil appeals, and 77 district courts.

District courts in Oklahoma may hear almost any type of case. This means they may hear **criminal cases, civil cases,** and cases involving young people, traffic offenses, and small claims of less than $3,000. The district courts hear jury trials. District judges are elected on a **non-partisan** basis to four-year terms.

The Oklahoma Supreme Court meets on the second floor of the capitol building in Oklahoma City.

The court of civil appeals reviews cases that have been heard in a district court. Cases are assigned to the court of civil appeals by the supreme court. Twelve judges from seven districts serve on the court of civil appeals. Appellate judges are appointed by the governor for a six-year term.

Unlike most states, Oklahoma has two courts of last resort—the supreme court and the court of **criminal** appeals. The court of criminal appeals hears all cases involving crimes and is the court of last resort for criminal cases. It also hears cases involving the death penalty. Five judges serve on the court of criminal appeals, and they are appointed by the governor.

The supreme court has the final say on all civil cases that are appealed. It may overrule decisions of the court of civil appeals. Certain cases may also start in the supreme court. The nine judges who serve on the supreme court are appointed by the governor.

The Cherokee National Capital

Tahlequah, in northeastern Oklahoma, is the oldest established community in the state. In 1839, the leaders of the Cherokee nation set up a government there. They built a capitol, a prison, and schools. Tahlequah still serves as the capital of the Cherokee nation.

Oklahoma's Culture

Oklahoma's culture is unique blend of Native American traditions, the cowhand lifestyle, and big city commotion.

NATIVE AMERICAN LEGACY

Oklahoma is proud of its Native American **heritage.** Oklahoma has the largest Native American population of any state in the United States. Many of the 250,000 Native American living in Oklahoma are descended from the 67 tribes that inhabited the Indian Territory.

The Red Earth Festival, held in Oklahoma City each June, is the largest Native American cultural and arts show in the world. More than 2,000 Native American artists, dancers, and singers from more than 100 tribes across North America participate. One of the festival's goals is to highlight the **diversity** of the Native American cultures. Visitors come from all over the United States to learn about the culture of the first Americans.

Oklahoma celebrates its Native American heritage on its license plates.

THE OLD WEST

The Big Country Weekend, held in Vinita every September, celebrates the state's old west heritage. Visitors enjoy bull-riding contests, cattle-roping events, country and western music concerts, dancing, and plenty of food.

Held every April, the '89er Celebration commemorates the Land Run of 1889 and the birth of the town of Guthrie. Celebration events include the state's largest '89er Day Parade and a Wild West rodeo at the Lazy E Arena. Visitors can also enjoy **chuck wagon** food and the carnival, complete with rides and attractions.

The Oklahoma State Fair, held every September in Oklahoma City, brings more than a million visitors to the state. The fair's food is a major attraction, and fairgoers eat more than 80,000 corn dogs, 54,000 tacos, and 50,000 cinnamon rolls. Visitors enjoy all types of entertainment—livestock contests, pig races, a petting zoo, pony and camel rides, craft shows, and carnival attractions. The championship rodeo includes cowboys and cowgirls competing in a number of events, including saddle bronco riding, bareback riding, barrel racing, steer wrestling, and calf roping.

CITY CELEBRATIONS

Oklahoma City holds the Festival of the Arts each April. Founded in 1967, the festival brings more than 700,000 people to the city each year. The festival is one of the top fine arts festivals in the nation, highlighting all types of art. More than 150 artists, photographers, and sculptors come to Oklahoma City from all over the country. The festival features four stages of dance, theater, and other performing arts.

The city of Norman holds an annual May Fair Arts Festival. Visitors can view the works of more than 100 fine artists, quality craft workers, and Native American **artisans.** A special exhibit allows visitors to see metal workers turn 22-pound blocks of solid metal into **molten** liquid, then pour the metal, let it cool, and work it until a piece of art takes shape.

Oklahoma's Food

Oklahoma's Official State Meal was determined by the state legislature in 1988. The meal includes a large menu that reflects Oklahoma's cultural backgrounds, the state's history, and farming today. Meats include barbecued pork, chicken-fried steak, and sausage with biscuits and gravy. Vegetables include fried okra and squash, grits, corn, and black-eyed peas. Breads include cornbread and biscuits. Dessert consists of strawberries and pecan pie.

BARBECUE

Barbeques are popular throughout Oklahoma. In many towns, barbecues and chili cook-offs are important

Barbeques and chili cook-offs are popular events in Oklahoma.

Buffalo Chili

Buffalo chili is a thick, hearty dish. **Be sure to have an adult help you with this recipe.**

1 lb. ground bison
1 medium onion, chopped
1 15 ounce can pinto beans, rinsed and drained
2 16 ounce cans peeled tomatoes
1/2 cup water
2 teaspoons chili powder
1/2 teaspoon ground cumin
1/2 teaspoon salt
1/2 teaspoon ground pepper
1/4 cup fresh cilantro, chopped

In a nonstick skillet, sauté the ground bison and onion until the meat is browned and the onion is tender. Add the pinto beans, tomatoes, water, and seasonings. Cover and simmer for one hour, adding more water if the chili becomes too thick. Add chopped cilantro and simmer an additional 10 minutes. Spoon into bowls and garnish with grated cheese or diced jalapeño peppers.

events, and people look forward to compete in these events each year. Two well-known events are the Ponca City Chili Cook-Off and Barbecue and the Chili Cook-off and Classic Car Show in Arrowhead.

Oklahoma's Folklore and Legends

Legends and folklore are stories that are not totally true, but are often based on bits of truth. These stories help people understand things that cannot be easily explained. They also teach lessons to younger generations. Oklahoma is rich in cowhand and Native American legends. Cowhands are known for telling tall tales around campfires. Native Americans often tell stories about their values and their love of nature.

SPANISH TREASURE

Native Americans who live near the town of Vici, in eastern Ellis County, tell a story about buried Spanish treasure. They say that long ago Spanish explorers passed through the area with several **burros** loaded with gold. The native people and the Spanish explorers fought for the gold, but the Spanish buried the gold before the Native Americans won the battle. In 1912, several small Spanish coins were found near Vici. However, to this day, no one has found the buried treasure.

A NATIVE AMERICAN ROSE

In 1838, the Cherokee were forced to move westward along the Trail of Tears. The mothers of the Cherokee were grieving and crying so much, they were unable to help their children survive the long journey. The tribal elders prayed for a sign that would lift the mothers' spirits to give them strength. The next day a beautiful wild rose began to grow where each of the mothers' tears fell. The rose is white for their tears, its gold center repre-

sents the gold taken from Cherokee lands, and seven leaves on each stem stand for the seven Cherokee clans. The wild Cherokee rose grows along the route of the Trail of Tears into eastern Oklahoma.

OKLAHOMA WEATHER

The weather in Oklahoma is subject to extremes. Instead of rainstorms, Oklahoma gets dust storms. On the same day, one man can suffer from sunstroke at noon, while his neighbor can freeze later that night. But the temperature is not the state's only weather phenomenon. The winds in Oklahoma are noteworthy, too. People have a crowbar hole drilled through an outside wall, which they use to test the wind. They stick a crowbar through the hole, and if it bends, then the wind is normal. But if the crowbar breaks, well, then it's best to stay inside until the wind dies down.

Oklahoma's Sports Teams

Although Oklahoma does not have any major league professional sports teams, many Oklahomans enjoy following minor league teams and college sports.

THE OKLAHOMA REDHAWKS

The Oklahoma Redhawks play minor league baseball as part of the Pacific Coast League. In 2003, the Redhawks, under manager Bobby Jones, finished with a record of 70 wins and 72 losses. The Redhawks are associated with the Texas Rangers of Major League Baseball. The Redhawks play in the SBC Bricktown Ballpark in Oklahoma City. The ballpark was built to resemble famous old-time ballparks with low outfield walls and seats that are close to the field.

Redhawks baseball draws fans to Oklahoma City.

The OU Sooners football team is a state-wide favorite.

COLLEGE SPORTS

The University of Oklahoma is well known for football. On January 1, 2003, the Oklahoma Sooners won the National Collegiate Athletic Association (NCAA) Rose Bowl in Pasadena, California. They

Barry Sanders's NCAA Rushing Record

In 1988 Barry Sanders, a running back for Oklahoma State, had a great season. He set an NCAA rushing record of 2,628 yards. That year he rushed for 39 touchdowns and four 300-yard games. Sanders rushed for more yards in one season than many teams do. Sanders played for the Detroit Lions, where he became the National Football League's third all-time leading rusher.

Rodeo fans from across the country gather for the excitement of the International Finals.

beat Washington State with a score of 34–14. The Sooners played in their first college bowl game in 1939. That year they lost to Tennessee with a score of 17–0. The Sooners have played in the Sugar Bowl in New Orleans five times, and they are the only team to have played in the Sugar Bowl three years in a row, from 1949–1951. The Sooners have won seven national championships. Only Notre Dame, Alabama, and Michigan have won more.

INTERNATIONAL FINALS RODEO

The International Finals Rodeo has been called the Super Bowl of rodeos because it is the biggest rodeo event in the United States. Sponsored by the International Professional Rodeo Association, based in Oklahoma City, rodeo participants train all year for the event. Events include saddle and bareback riding, bull riding, calf roping, steer wrestling, and cowgirl barrel racing.

Oklahoma's Businesses and Products

Agriculture, oil, and machinery manufacturing are important industries in Oklahoma. These industries help support the state by offering jobs to many people.

FARM PRODUCTS

About 34 million acres of Oklahoma's land is devoted to agriculture. The average size of a farm in Oklahoma is 405 acres. Winter wheat, hay, corn for grain, peanuts, and pecans are the top Oklahoma crops. Oklahoma ranks second in the nation in the production of winter wheat, third in the production of pecans, third in the production of rye, sixth in the production of grain sorghum, seventh in peanuts, and tenth in peaches. Oklahoma produces more than 150 million bushels of winter wheat and 63 million pounds of pecans each year.

Wheat farms stretch across much of Oklahoma's landscape.

Oklahoma is also a leading livestock state. The state has about 5.2 million cattle, 55,000 sheep, 5.3 million chickens, 2.26 million hogs, and 170,000 horses. Oklahoma ranks fourth in the nation in cattle and calf production, sixth in hog production, and eighth in broiler production.

Oklahoma's first oil boom began in the early 1900s, just before statehood.

Oklahoma beef cattle, hogs, and sheep produce about one billion pounds of meat per year. Oklahoma poultry produce 945 million eggs per year.

OIL AND GAS

Petroleum is Oklahoma's number-one industry, employing about 50,000 people and contributing millions of dollars each year to the state's economy. For example, oil-generated revenue provided more than $150 million for education in Oklahoma. About 750,000 oil wells have been drilled in the state, including those that stand on the state's capital grounds. Oklahoma ranks second only to Texas in the number of active oil wells. Oklahoma ranks fifth in oil production among the states.

Oklahoma ranks fourth among the states in natural gas production. Natural gas supplies about 33 percent of the energy in the state.

MANUFACTURING

Oklahoma is a leading manufacturer of transportation equipment, machinery, electronics, plastics, food products, and metal products.

Attractions and Landmarks

Oklahoma offers people many places to visit. Some of its major attractions are historical sites found throughout the state.

FORT WASHITA

The U.S. Army established Fort Washita near Madill in 1841. This fort was built in south-central Oklahoma to protect the Native Americans who had recently been moved to the Indian Territory from other areas. During the **Civil War** (1861–1865), the fort was occupied by Confederate soldiers from Texas. Today the Oklahoma Historical Society maintains the Fort Washita site. Visitors are offered tours along cobblestone walkways throughout the fort. They can also enjoy living-history exhibits and reenactments with men and women dressed in period clothes.

Visitors to Fort Washita can explore the ruins of the West Barracks, where soldiers once lived. They can also tour the restored South Barracks to see how troops lived in the 1800s.

GUTHRIE

Guthrie, in north-central Oklahoma, was established in a few hours during the first **land rush** in 1889. Guthrie became the capital of the Oklahoma Territory, and in 1907, it became the first capital of the state. The downtown historic district has been restored to show many storefronts and residences from the time when Guthrie was the capital of Oklahoma. Visitors can ride a trolley through the historic district and learn more about Guthrie's Wild West history. Guthrie's Lazy E Arena holds more than 25 championship rodeo events each year.

OKLAHOMA CITY

The National Cowboy and Western Heritage Museum, located in Oklahoma City, is dedicated to the West's heritage. Visitors can see exhibits on ranching, hear western musical performances, and experience a **chuck wagon** gathering. Also at the museum is the Prosperity Junction display, a replica of a late 1800s western cattle town. Buildings at Prosperity Junction include a stable, blacksmith shop, train depot, saloon, school, and marshal's office. The museum has many galleries of western art and sculpture.

Oklahoma City visitors also can view the Oklahoma City National Memorial, which pays tribute to the 168 people who were killed on April 19, 1995, when the Alfred P. Murrah federal

Oklahoma City National Memorial pays solemn tribute to the 168 victims of the bombing.

building was bombed. The memorial stands on the site of the Murrah building. On April 19, 2000, President Bill Clinton dedicated the memorial in downtown Oklahoma City.

The unique National Softball Hall of Fame and Museum honors softball greats.

The National Softball Hall of Fame and Museum is also located in Oklahoma City. Exhibits tell the history of amateur softball and feature some of the sport's great players. One of the first players honored was Jim Ramage, a shortstop from Paducah, Kentucky. Ramage was voted into the hall of fame in 1961.

Gene Autry

In the town of Gene Autry, residents and visitors celebrate the Gene Autry Oklahoma Film and Music Festival. Every September, people come to enjoy exhibits

Music fans of all ages come to Gene Autry every September to enjoy the music of singing cowhands.

Places to See in Oklahoma

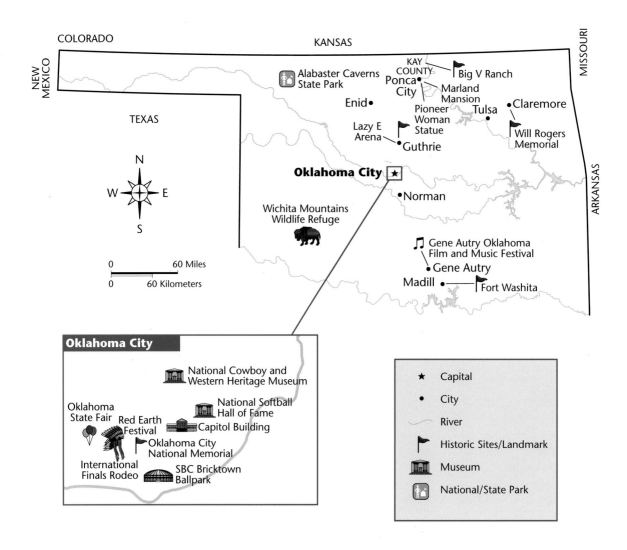

dedicated to singing cowboys. Gene Autry, Roy Rogers, Dale Evans, and other western stars are honored at the museum. Visitors listen to country-and-western music, dance, and enjoy western barbeque.

PONCA CITY

A huge mansion built by Ernst Whitworth Marland stands in Ponca City. The mansion is located in a clearing and is almost completely surrounded by water. Marland established the Marland Oil Company, and in the 1920s, his company controlled one-tenth of the world's

Alabaster Caverns State Park

The largest **gypsum** cave in the world is located in Alabaster Caverns State Park. The cave is three-fourths of a mile long. Inside the cave, the walls are pink-colored alabaster, which is a fine-grained gypsum. Some people come to see the bats in the alabaster caves. Five species of bats live there. The caves provide the bats shelter during the day.

oil supply. Marland later served as Oklahoma's governor from 1935 to 1939.

Located on eight acres in the middle of Ponca City, Marland's 22-room mansion became famous for its well-crafted gardens. On the grounds of the estate stands a seventeen-foot-tall statue of a pioneer woman holding the hand of a young boy. Both are dressed in traditional pioneer clothing. Marland wanted to represent a group of people whom he called "America's vanishing people"—pioneer women. Today, visitors can tour the mansion's grounds, which include the gardens, a stable, an artist's studio, a boathouse, and other buildings.

Sculptor Bryant Baker created the Pioneer Woman Statue in 1929. He beat out eleven other sculptors to win the opportunity to make the monument.

KAY COUNTY

In Kay County, William H. Vanselous established the Big V ranch during a 1893 land rush. What began as a 160-acre land grab became one of the nation's largest mule ranches. The Big V ranch also boasts an annual corn harvest of 100,000 bushels. The ranch eventually had its own power plant for its 45 miles of electrified fence. The Big V ranch house, built in 1908, is listed on the National Register of Historic Places. Visitors to Oklahoma can tour the ranch house and the Big V grounds.

CLAREMORE

The Will Rogers Memorial in Claremore is dedicated to telling the story of the actor and humorist Will Rogers. Rogers purchased the twenty-acre site in 1911 and had planned to retire there. After his death in 1935, his family donated the land for the memorial. Visitors to the memorial can see the museum with thousands of Rogers's photographs and letters, as well as art and sculptures by western artists. Will Rogers's family tomb is located on the grounds of the memorial.

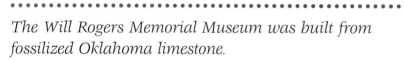

The Will Rogers Memorial Museum was built from fossilized Oklahoma limestone.

Map of Oklahoma

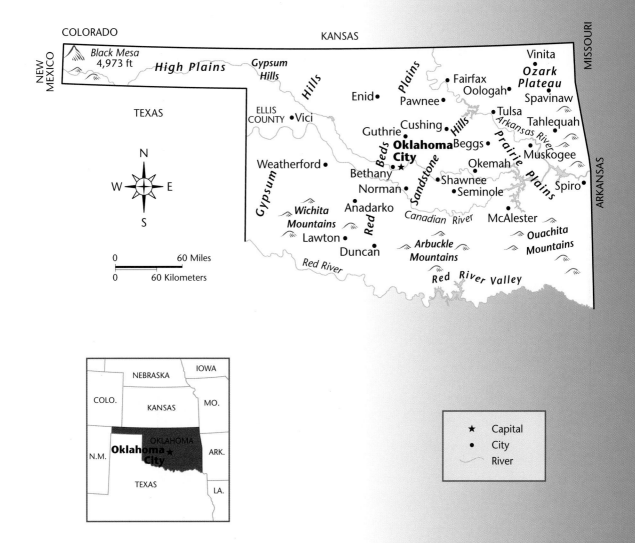

COLORADO

KANSAS

MISSOURI

NEW MEXICO

Black Mesa
4,973 ft

High Plains

Gypsum Hills

Vinita

Ozark Plateau

• Fairfax

Oologah•

Spavinaw

• Pawnee

Hills

Enid•

Plains

•Tulsa

Tahlequah

TEXAS

ELLIS COUNTY

•Vici

Guthrie•

Cushing•

Arkansas River

Hills

Oklahoma City

Beggs

Muskogee•

Prairie Plains

Beds

Weatherford•

Bethany

★

Sandstone

• Okemah

•Shawnee

Spiro•

ARKANSAS

Norman•

•Seminole

Gypsum

Red

• Anadarko

Canadian River

McAlester•

Wichita Mountains

Arbuckle Mountains

Ouachita Mountains

Lawton •

Duncan

Red River

Red River Valley

N
W — E
S

0   60 Miles

0   60 Kilometers

NEBRASKA

IOWA

COLO.

KANSAS

MO.

N.M.

Oklahoma City

OKLAHOMA ★

ARK.

TEXAS

LA.

★   Capital
•   City
   River

45

Glossary

archaeological of or related to the study of ancient peoples

archaeologists social scientists who study the cultural remains of ancient people

artisans artists and craftspeople

atomic cannon a mobile cannon capable of launching a nuclear weapon

bill a proposed law

burros small donkeys used to carry heavy loads

chuck wagon a wagon that served food to cowhands and settlers during long journeys

civil cases court actions between individuals having to do with private rights rather than criminal action

Civil War the war between the northern states, called the Union, and the southern states, known as the Confederacy, fought between 1861 and 1865

constitution a plan of government

criminal of or relating to committing a crime

criminal cases court actions dealing with violations of the law

diversity distinctive, different, having variety

drought a long period of time without rain or snow

erosion the wearing away of land by wind, water, or cold

extinct no longer living

federal government the national government of the United States, located in Washington, D.C.

gypsum a naturally occurring form of calcium sulfate, often used in cement, paint, and other products

heritage traditions passed down from previous generations

humid damp or moist

land lottery a method of settling land in which the government chooses names in a drawing

land rush a method of settling disputed lands in Oklahoma

legislature group of elected officials who make laws

Louisiana Territory a large section of land between the Mississippi River and the Rocky Mountains that was purchased from France in 1803. This land doubled the size of the United States.

mammoths a prehistoric, elephant-like mammal with long, wooly hair

molten melted rock or metal

non-partisan an election in which the candidates do not belong to political parties

parasite a plant or animal that lives off another plant or animal

pelts animal fur

plains   flat land surfaces

plateau   a broad, level, flat, elevated area of land; a tableland

pollination   the transfer of pollen from a male flower to a female flower, which causes flowers to bloom

prairie   a large area of level, grassy ground

Pulitzer Prize   a well-known prize awarded for outstanding writing or journalism

retention ballot   a type of ballot on which a voter indicates whether a judge should stay in office

survey   to measure a parcel of land

terrorism   the use of violence for political purposes

More Books to Read

Baldwin, Guy. *Oklahoma.* New York: Benchmark Books, 2001.

Boraas, Tracy. *Oklahoma.* Mankato, Minn.: Capstone Press, 2004.

Durrett, Deane. *Oklahoma.* San Diego, Calif.: Kidhaven Press, 2003.

Lamb, Nancy. *One April Morning: Children Remember the Oklahoma City Bombing.* New York: Lothrop, Lee & Shepard Books, 1996.

Saylor-Marchant, Linda. *Oklahoma.* New York: Children's Press, 2003.

Index

About the Authors

Reuben Anderson spent his early years in the suburbs of Tulsa, Oklahoma. Although he currently lives in Minnesota, he has fond memories of his Oklahoma childhood.

D. J. Ross is a writer and educator with more than 30 years of experience in education. He has lived throughout the United States and has often visited Oklahoma. He now lives in the Midwest with his three basset hounds.